LOGIC COUNTDOWN

Grades 3–4

Written by Bonnie Risby

Illustrated by Dean Crawford

10·9·8·7..

First published in 2005 by Prufrock Press Inc.

Published in 2021 by Routledge
605 Third Avenue, New York, NY 10017
2 Park Square, Milton Park, Abingdon, Oxon OX14 4RN

Routledge is an imprint of the Taylor & Francis Group, an informa business.

Copyright © 2005, Taylor & Francis Group.

ISBN-13: 978-1-5936-3087-4 (pbk)

DOI: 10.4324/9781003236252

Contents

Logic Countdown

Lesson	Common Core State Standards
Relationships (Lessons 1-7)	ELA-Literacy: L.3.5 & L.4.5 Demonstrate understanding of figurative language, word relationships and nuances in word meanings.
Analogies (Lessons 8-18)	Math: 3.G.A Reason with shapes and their attributes. 4.OA.C Generate and analyze patterns. ELA-Literacy: L.3.5 & L.4.5 Demonstrate understanding of figurative language, word relationships and nuances in word meanings.
Sequencing (Lessons 19-25)	Math: 4.OA.C & 5.OA.B Generate and analyze patterns.
All and No Statements (Lessons 26-28)	ELA/Literacy: CCRA.R.8 Delineate and evaluate the argument and specific claims in a text, including the validity of the reasoning as well as the relevance and sufficiency of the evidence.
Syllogisms (Lessons 29-34)	ELA/Literacy: CCRA.R.8 Delineate and evaluate the argument and specific claims in a text, including the validity of the reasoning as well as the relevance and sufficiency of the evidence.
If-Then Statements (Lessons 35-37)	ELA/Literacy: CCRA.R.8 Delineate and evaluate the argument and specific claims in a text, including the validity of the reasoning as well as the relevance and sufficiency of the evidence.
Deduction (Lessons 38-46)	ELA/Literacy: RF.K.1 & RF.1.1 Demonstrate understanding of the organization and basic features of print. RF.K.3, RF.1.3, & RF.2.3 Know and apply grade-level phonics and word analysis skills in decoding words. RF.1.4 & RF.2.4 Read with sufficient accuracy and fluency to support comprehension.
Inferencing (Lessons 47-54)	ELA/Literacy: L.3.5 & L.4.5 Demonstrate understanding of figurative language, word relationships, and nuances in word meanings.

For the Instructor

Children have a natural love of games and puzzles. This book taps this fascination with puzzles. It is designed to titillate children's imaginations and at the same time sharpen their logical thinking skills.

Through *Logic Countdown* youngsters encounter the thinking methods perfected by the ancients, realizing only that they're experiencing new adventures in the strategies of puzzle solving.

The activities in this book fall into six broad categories. These categories are adapable to small groups or individual work, and include the following:
- relationships
- analogies
- sequences
- syllogisms
- deductions
- inferences

The skills students build by using this book are applicable to several areas of the curriculum. Academic skills used for reading, math, writing, and science all depend on the ability to perceive and define relationships and to form inferences. But beyond the academic world, students will find logical thinking an integral part of everyday life. These are skills that allow students to analyze situations, see relationships, organize information, and draw generalizations. As students develop their logical thinking skills, expect them to approach all information with critical forethought.

The instructor is the most important element for making logic palatable and exciting to young thinkers. It is the instructor's role to not only present the process for solving the puzzles but also to build an atmosphere that encourages analytical thinking. Since the thought process itself is more valuable than the answers listed in the back of the book, it is very important to compare and discuss methods of arriving at conclusions and to be tolerant of creative diversions from the norm. Though the material in this book is presented in a sequential manner, it is suggested that each new type of logic problem be presented and discussed and sample problems be worked together before students are allowed to work independently. By discussing the puzzles, students will be able to learn a generalized thinking process instead of having to tackle each problem as a unique entity.

Logic Countdown is the first in a three-part series of logic books for students in grades three through seven. Once students have mastered the skills presented in this book, they will be ready to meet new challenges with *Logic Liftoff* and *Orbiting with Logic*. Are you ready to begin this exciting logic adventure with your students? Then begin the countdown—10, 9, 8, 7...

Name _____

Look carefully at the four items in each group. They are all related in one way. On the line, write how the four things are related.

1. yellow, red, blue, orange _____

2. triangle, square, rectangle, pentagon _____

3. cup, gallon, quart, pint _____

4. Spain, France, Italy, Sweden _____

5. book, poster, tablet, envelope _____

6. scissors, knife, saw, razor blade _____

7. salt, sugar, flour, soda _____

8. licorice, chocolate, peppermint, vanilla _____

9. oak, pine, poplar, hemlock _____

10. Atlanta, Chicago, Seattle, Houston _____

11. cup, vase, bucket, pot _____

12. cake, cookies, candy, ice cream _____

Name_____

Look carefully at the three things in each group. Decide how these things are related. Then add one more thing to the list that will fit into this relationship.

1. wheat, rice, barley _____

2. coat, shirt, pants _____

3. milk, water, coffee _____

4. Wednesday, Tuesday, Friday _____

5. bluejay, robin, hawk _____

6. train, airplane, car _____

7. book, paper, pencil _____

8. grass, dollar bill, shamrock _____

9. apple, cherry, tangerine _____

10. Valentine's Day, Easter, Hanukkah _____

11. Julie, Kimberly, Veronica _____

Make your own list of four related items.

12. _____

13. _____

Name _____

Look carefully at the four items in each group. Decide how the four
things are related. Then add one other item that will also fit into this
relationship.

1. peach, cherry, olive, avocado _____

2. apple, pear, peach, watermelon _____

3. baseball, soccer, polo, football _____

4. pine, lime, pea, spinach _____

5. orange, marble, baseball, globe _____

6. sugar, jam, honey, molasses _____

7. skateboard, car, bicycle, cart _____

8. sunshine, rain, fog, wind _____

9. daffodil, lemon, banana, canary _____

10. carrots, potatoes, beets, onions _____

11. bee, fly, dragonfly, mosquito _____

12. chocolate, mud, football, nut _____

Name_____

This is your chance to be both a creative and critical thinker. Here are several categories. On the lines under each heading, write four or more things that fit into these categories.

Cities in your state you have never visited

_____   _____

_____   _____

Boys names that begin with _B_

_____   _____

_____   _____

Things that are good to eat and good for you

_____   _____

_____   _____

Things that are shaped like a circle

_____   _____

_____   _____

Things that start with the letter j and are found in the house

_____   _____

_____   _____

Things that are white and soft

_____   _____

_____   _____

Things that come in pairs and are used by children

_____   _____

_____   _____

Things that are sticky

_____   _____

_____   _____

Things the have two syllables and are found in a school desk

_____   _____

_____   _____

Name_____

Here are lists of things that certain people like. Look for the relationship between the things that they like. Write the common characteristic of all of the things each person likes.

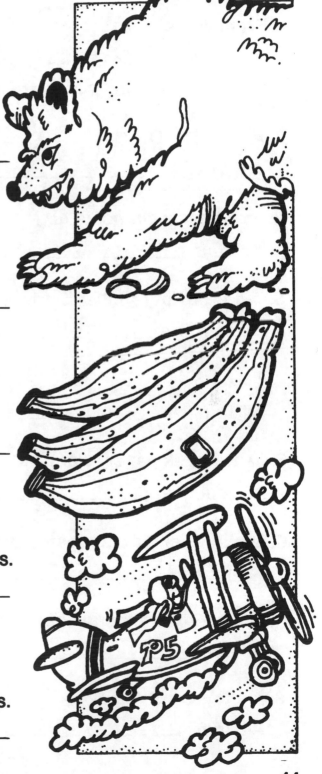

1. Julian likes chocolate but not peppermint.
   Julian likes dirt but not grass.
   Julian likes bark but not leaves.
   Julian likes grizzly bears but not polar bears.

   Julian likes _____

2. Sam likes oranges but not bananas.
   Sam likes baseballs but not footballs.
   Sam likes marbles but not jacks.
   Sam likes stop lights but not stop signs.

   Sam likes _____

3. Mike likes bananas but not grapes.
   Mike likes lemons but not limes.
   Mike likes daffodils but not violets.
   Mike likes canaries but not sparrows.

   Mike likes _____

4. Jill likes robins but not penguins.
   Jill likes airplanes but not trains.
   Jill likes kites but not kingpins.
   Jill likes boomerangs but not bumper stickers.

   Jill likes _____

5. John likes bowling but not baseball.
   John likes math but not recess.
   John likes cleaning but not weeding.
   John likes coffee tables but not picnic tables.

   John likes _____

Name_____

Look carefully at the five items in each group. Decide what the
relationship is for the items in each group. Decide which thing does
not belong with the others. Circle the thing that does not belong. Tell
how the other four things are related.

Example:

All four things are made of straight lines.

1. A   E   N   O   U

All four _____

2. cow tiger robin horse dog

All four _____

3. Ted Lisa Katy Amber Cindy

All four are _____

4. 7 2 8 14 6

All four are _____

5. pencil book paper ruler milk

All four are _____

6. apple peach potato pear grapes

All four _____

7. strawberry cranberry cherry banana apple

All four _____

8. A N O Z E

All four _____

Name_____

Look carefully at the five items in each group. Decide what the relationship is for each group. Decide which thing does not belong with the others. Circle the thing that does not belong. Tell how the other four things are related.

1.

   All four are _____

2.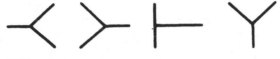

   All four are _____

3.

   All four are _____

4.

   All four are _____

5. see taste hear smell tired

   All four are _____

6. Jupiter Saturn moon Pluto Uranus

   All four are _____

7. pizza gumdrops lollipops ice cream cookies

   All four are _____

8. flour pepper sugar salt soda

   All four are _____

9. 1 cent 5 cents 15 cents 25 cents 10 cents

   All four are _____

Name _____

Analogies are comparisons between two things. They point out ways that the two things are similar. Finish the following analogies by choosing the set of pictures that best completes each sentence. Then write the correct letter in the space.

Example: **A** is like **a** as **B** is like **b**

___ 1. (fish) is like (fish) as

   a. ↑ is like ↓

   b. (flower) is like (flower)

   c. (paper) is like (paper)

___ 4. (apple) is like (pumpkin) as

   a. (hat) is like (ghost)

   b. (tie) is like (bow)

   c. (sunglasses) is like (glasses)

___ 2. (cup) is like (cup) as

   a. (apple) is like (apple)

   b. (cone) is like (cone)

   c. ◯ is like (baseball)

___ 5. (spade) is like (spade) as

   a. ☐ is like (cube)

   b. ◇ is like (diamond)

   c. (umbrella) is like (umbrella)

___ 3. (arrow) is like (trident) as

   a. (moon) is like (moon)

   b. ◯ is like ⊕

   c. (rectangle) is like (window)

___ 6. ☐ is like (square with dot) as

   a. ◯ is like ◯

   b. ◯ is like (filled circle)

   c. ◯ is like (circle with dot)

Name_____

Finish the following analogies by choosing the set of pictures or
figures that best completes each sentence. Then write the correct
letter in the space.

Example: **T** is like ⊢ as **W** is like **ξ**

___ 1.   ↑ is like ↓ as

    a.   → is like ←

    b.   ↗ is like ↖

    c.   → is like ↓

___ 2.   ☆ is like ✪ as

    a.   ♥ is like ♠

    b.   ✚ is like ✖

    c.   ▲ is like ◪

___ 3.   C,D,E is like 1,2,3 as

    a.   G,H,I is like 7,8,9

    b.   X,Y,Z is like 14,13,12

    c.   13,15,17 is like A,B,C

___ 4.   **N** is like **N** as

    a.   **C** is like **C**

    b.   **H** is like **H**

    c.   **Z** is like **Z**

___ 5.    ⊞ is like ⊞ as

    a.    ○ is like ◒

    b.    ⊕ is like ⊕

    c.    ⊕ is like ✳

___ 6.    ☀ is like ○ as

    a.    △ is like △

    b. 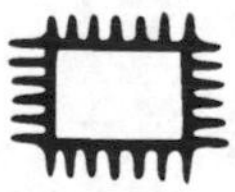   ▢ is like □

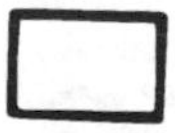

    c.    ○ is like ☼

Name_____

Finish the following analogies by choosing the set of words, numbers, or figures that best completes each sentence. Then write the correct letter in the space. Notice that we have written the analogies in a new form.

"3 : 9 as 10 : 30" means "3 is to 9 as 10 is to 30"
or "3 is related to 9 in the same way 10 is related to 30."

5. 10 9 8 : 9 8 7 as 5 4 3 : _____
   a) 324   b) 432   c) 456   d) 765

6. LIVE : EVIL as 3249 : _____
   a) 2496   b) 3294   c) 8563   d) 9423

7. 5 : 10 as 10 : _____
   a) 15   b) 5   c) 25   d) 2

1. 5 : 6 as 7 : _____
   a) 4   b) 9   c) 6   d) 8

2. 4 : 8 as 5 : _____
   a) 5   b) 8   c) 10   d) 15

8. 5 cents : 50 cents as 10 cents : _____
   a) 65 cents   b) 100 cents
   c) 25 cents   d) 55 cents

3. ABC : CBA as MNO : _____
   a) PQR   b) DEF   c)NOM   d)ONM

9. north : south as east : _____
   a) west   b) northeast
   c) direction   d) north

4. ABC : BCD as OPQ : _____
   a) PQO   b) PQR   c) RST   D) QPO

10. 30 : 40 as 40 : _____
   a) 80   b) 60   c) 50   d) 20

16

Name_____

Finish the following statements by choosing the word that best completes each analogy. Remember to consider carefully the relationship between the first two members of the analogy. Then look for the same relationship between the second two members of the analogy. Write the letter of the correct answer in the space.

Example: Robin is to bird as shark is to fish.

1. Swift is to rapid as small is to _____

    a. mouse   b. little   c. rush   d. large

2. Cod is to trout as grouse is to _____

    a. covey   b. bird   c. fish   d. egret

3. Silver is to metal as Irish Setter is to _____

    a. red   b. curry   c. dog   d. collie

4. Stalk is to leopard as slither is to _____

    a. slender   b. crawl   c. slippery   d. snake

5. Jump is to feet as blink is to _____

    a. eyes   b. toes   c. wink   d. ink

6. King is to queen as prince is to _____

    a. throne   b. power   c. princess   d. royalty

7. Flock is to sheep as herd is to _____

    a. heard   b. group   c. cattle   d. ducks

8. Nervous is to calm as cautious is to _____

    a. wary   b. careless   c. fox   d. carton

9. Calf is to cow as kitten is to _____

    a. fuzzy   b. mitten   c. purr   d. cat

10. Granite is to rock as Illinois is to _____

    a. Indiana   b. state   c. Springfield   d. Chicago

Name_____

Finish the following statements by choosing the word that best completes the analogy. Remember to consider carefully the relationship between the first two members of the analogy. Then look for the same relationship between the second two members of the analogy. Write the letter of the correct answer in the space.

Example: Leaf is to green as bark is to brown.

1. Car is to Ford as horse is to ____

   a. mammal   b. coral   c. saddle   d. palomino

2. Left is to right as straight is to ____

   a. strait   b. road   c. crooked   d. arrow

3. Herd is to elk as fleet is to ____

   a. feet   b. swift   c. commander   d. ship

4. Leopard is to cat as python is to ____

   a. poisonous   b. snake   c. cobra   d. slither

5. Rug is to carpet as pail is to ____

   a. water   b. pale   c. failure   d. bucket

6. Song is to ballad as shoe is to ____

   a. sandal   b. foot   c. scuffed   d. cobbler

7. Beggar is to poor as president is to ____

   a. chairman   b. leader   c. powerful   d. nation

8. Colt is to horse as puppy is to ____

   a. dog   b. puppies   c. fuzzy   d. Spot

9. Neat is to sloppy as take is to ____

   a. think   b. swallow   c. give   d. tack

10. Horse is to gallop as frog is to ____

   a. bull   b. green   c. pond   d. jump

Name_____

Finish the following statements by choosing the word that best completes the analogy. Remember to consider carefully the relationship between the first two members of the analogy. Then look for the same relationship between the second two members of the analogy. Write the letter of the correct answer in the space.

Example: Nose is to face as finger is to hand.

1. Noise is to sound as green is to _____

   a. grass   b. lime   c. color   d. cool

2. Red is to color as tuna is to _____

   a. fish   b. salmon   c. salad   d. swim

3. Bee is to cricket as corn is to _____

   a. green   b. wheat   c. cob   d. field

4. Turtle is to crawl as ball is to _____

   a. bawl   b. tennis   c. bounce   d. bat

5. Rock is to stone as moist is to _____

   a. damp   b. dry   c. ship   d. arid

6. World Series is to baseball as Super Bowl is to _____

   a. team   b. game   c. football   d. touchdown

7. Animal is to antelope as tree is to _____

   a. leaf   b. sap   c. maple   d. lumber

8. Safe is to hazardous as beautiful is to _____

   a. soft   b. adorn   c. beast   d. ugly

9. Person is to multitude as quail is to _____

   a. bird   b. covey   c. dog   d. quaint

10. Photograph is to camera as newspaper is to _____

   a. read   b. boy   c. printing press   d. route

Name_____

Finish the following statements by choosing the word that best completes the analogy. Remember to consider carefully the relationship between the first two members of the analogy. Then look for the same relationship between the second two members of the analogy. Write the letter of the correct answer in the space.

Example: Fragile is to glass as flexible is to rubber.

1. Delicate is to coarse as simple is to _____

a. easy   b. sample   c. complex   d. elementary

2. Boa constrictor is to snake as carp is to _____

a. fish   b. perch   c. bass   d. hook

3. Page is to book as card is to _____

a. cart   b. deal   c. deck   d. ace

4. Marsh is to swamp as stratum is to _____

a. layer   b. status   c. bog   d. dig

5. Run is to deer as hop is to _____

a. foot   b. jump   c. rabbit   d. skip

6. Mineral is to salt as plant is to _____

a. flower   b. fragrance   c. garden   d. honeysuckle

7. Glass is to transparent as wood is to _____

a. trees   b. opaque   c. table   d. grain

8. Breathe is to respire as bubbly is to _____

a. bubbles   b. effervescent   c. soap   d. champagne

9. Basement is to building as foot is to _____

a. walk   b. toe   c. body   d. feet

10. Teacher is to school as doctor is to _____

a. medical   b. hospital   c. intern   d. medicine

Name_____

Finish the following statements by choosing the word that best completes the analogy. Remember to consider carefully the relationship between the first two members of the analogy. Then look for the same relationship between the second two members of the analogy. Write the letter of the correct answer in the space.

1. Nickel is to penny as ace is to _____

    a. dime   b. card   c. king   d. diamond

2. Foamy is to frothy as bloom is to _____

    a. petunia   b. fragrant   c. blossom   d. plant

3. Bunch is to banana as cluster is to _____

    a. yellow   b. custard   c. peaches   d. grapes

4. Marine animal is to manatee as bird is to _____

    a. nest   b. prey   c. falcon   d. talon

5. Peppermint is to spearmint as Cherokee is to _____

    a. tribe   b. Shoshone   c. headdress   d. brave

6. Agriculture is to farming as odor is to _____

    a. skunk   b. smell   c. melon   d. pine

7. Pyramid is to base as tree is to _____

    a. dogwood   b. grove   c. root   d. forest

8. Pride is to shame as friend is to _____

    a. foe   b. pal   c. fellow   d. sorrow

9. Doll is to dolls as woman is to _____

    a. girl   b. women   c. man   d. lady

10. f is to g as 6 is to _____

    a. h   b. six   c. 7   d. 5

Name_____

Finish the following statements by choosing the word that best completes the analogy. Remember to consider carefully the relationship between the first two members of the analogy. Then look for the same relationship between the second two members of the analogy. Write the letter of the correct answer in the space.

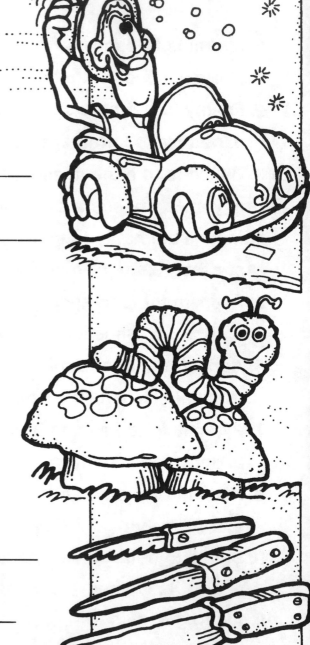

1. Chair is to leg as car is to _____

   a. road   b. truck   c. tire   d. drive

2. Strong is to weak as positive is to _____

   a. negative   b. district   c. clear   d. plain

3. Fragrance is to aroma as onlooker is to _____

   a. look   b. see   c. smell   d. observer

4. Clydesdale is to horse as centipede is to _____

   a. arthropod b. leg c. hundred d. century

5. Friday is to Saturday as June is to _____

   a. day   b. month   c. July   d. December

6. Pig is to hog as dog is to _____

   a. kennel   b. canine   c. bark   d. howl

7. Grape is to cluster as wolf is to _____

   a. prey   b. hunt   c. pack   d. cub

8. Wagons is to wagon as knives is to _____

   a. sharp   b. cut   c. carve   d. knife

9. Katydid is to grasshopper as aspen is to _____

   a. leaves   b. bark   c. poplar   d. log

10. Autumn is to winter as afternoon is to _____

   a. evening   b. morning   c. dawn   d. late

Name_____

Finish the following statements by choosing the word that best completes the analogy. Remember to consider carefully the relationship between the first two members of the analogy. Then look for the same relationship between the second two members of the analogy. Write the letter of the correct answer in the space.

1. City is to cities as ox is to _____

   a. yoke   b. wagon   c. oxen   d. ax

2. Rich is to poor as antique is to _____

   a. ancient   b. old   c. rusty   d. new

3. Brush is to painter as cleaver is to _____

   a. meat   b. clever   c. butcher   d. cut

4. Noisy is to boisterous as doubt is to _____

   a. believe   b. seek   c. mistrust   d. quiet

5. Pine is to cedar as Europe is to _____

   a. border   b. Paris   c. Atlantic   d. Asia

6. Tuesday is to day as tea is to _____

   a. lemon   b. beverage   c. coffee   d. sugar

7. Demonstrate is to show as attempt is to _____

   a. try   b. tease   c. shed   d. officer

8. Telephone is to ring as clock is to _____

   a. hand   b. face   c. chime   d. mantel

9. Steel is to bridge as china is to _____

   a. river   b. break   c. iron   d. platter

10. Shampoo is to hair as toothpaste is to _____

   a. teeth   b. brush   c. tube   d. floss

Name_____

This is your chance to write your own analogies. Look at the first two words and think about the relationship between them. Then find two other words with the same relationship that will complete the sentence. Be original and creative.

1. Pen is to paper as _____ is to _____

2. Cat is to fur as _____ is to _____

3. Sour is to pickle as _____ is to _____

4. City is to Los Angeles as _____ is to _____

5. Garage is to car as _____ is to _____

6. Collie is to dog as _____ is to _____

7. Net is to fisherman as _____ is to _____

8. Burn is to fire as _____ is to _____

9. Imitate is to mimic as _____ is to _____

10. Swift is to antelope as _____ is to _____

11. Popcorn is to salt as _____ is to _____

12. Grape is to cluster as _____ is to _____

13. Sheep is to wool as _____ is to _____

14. December is to month as _____ is to _____

15. Teacher is to student as _____ is to _____

Name_____

The following sets are in a logical sequence. Examine each set carefully and choose the item that should be the next in the set. Write the correct answer on the line.

1. 1, 3, 5, 7, 9, 11, _____
   a. 10   b. 13   c. 12   d. 14

2. 19, 28, 37, 46, 55, _____
   a. 76   b. 56   c. 66   d. 64

3. a, c, e, g, i, _____
   a. h   b. j   c. k   d. f

4. May, April, March, February, _____
   a. August   b. January   c. June
   d. December

5. dt, es, fr, gq, hp, _____
   a. jo   b. io   c. im   d. ia

6. 1, 7, 2, 7, 3, 7, 4, _____
   a. 5   b. 8   c. 7   d. 6

7. Monday, Wednesday, Friday, _____
   a. Sunday   b. Saturday
   c. Thursday   d. Tuesday

8. 1961, 1967, 1972, 1976, 1979, _____
   a. 1980   b. 1981   c. 1985   d. 1983

9. 1, two, 3, four, 5, _____
   a. six   b. five   c. 6   d. 7

10. penny, nickel, dime, _____
    a. 10   b. dollar   c. quarter   d. 25

11. 12:00, 12:15, 12:30, 12:45, _____
    a. 12:55   b. 1:30   c. 1:15   d. 1:00

12. 1/2, 1/4, 1/8, 1/16, _____
    a. 1/32   b. 2/4   c. 1/24   d. 1/64

13. a, b, b, b, c, b, d, b, _____
    a. b   b. f   c. e   d. h

14. 1, 2, 4, 7, 11, _____
    a. 15   b. 16   c. 14   d. 12

Name_____

The following sets are in a logical sequence. Examine each set carefully and choose the item that should be the next item in the set. Write the correct answer on the line.

1. 20, 22, 30, 33 , 40, 44, 50, _____
   a. 60   b. 53   c. 55   d. 54

2. I, III, V, VII, IX, _____
   a. X   b. XI   c. IV   d. XII

3. 1, 3, 6, 10, 15, _____
   a. 20   b. 21   c. 19   d. 16

4. May, June, July, August, _____
   a. September   b. October
   c. December   d. April

5. k, l, m, n, o, _____
   a. r   b. s   c. p   d. j

6. do, re, mi, _____
   a. so   b. la   c. fa   d. ti

7. 10%, 20%, 30%, 40%, _____
   a. 50 cents   b. $4.40   c. 50%
   d. 25%

8. 10, 9, 8, 7, 6, _____
   a. 7   b. 5   c. 4   d. 3

9. Z, Y, X, W, _____
   a. V   b. U   c. T   d. S

10. 2, 4, 6, 8, 10, _____
    a. 12   b. 11   c. 11½   d. 14

11. 98.6, 98.7, 98.8, 98.9, _____
    a. 98%   b. 98 cents   c. 99   d. 99.9

12. $1.50, $1.60, $1.70, $1.80, _____
    a. $.90   b. $1.40   c. 35 cents
    d. $1.90

Name_____

An Afternoon on Jerod's Island

Here are five statements dealing with *An Afternoon On Jerod's Island*. The statements, however, are not listed in the proper order. By reading the statements carefully, you can determine in what sequence they should occur. Once you have decided on the correct order, number the statements in the proper sequence. The first one is done for you.

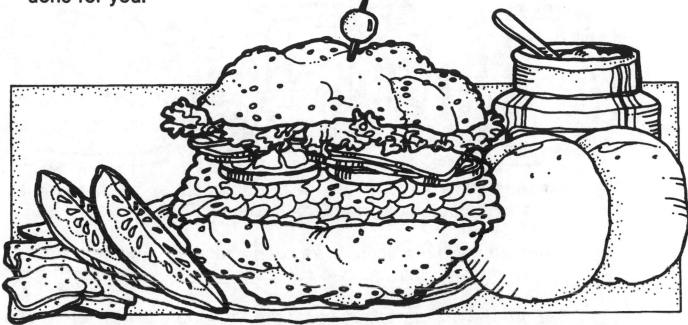

____ Ned, Bob, and Jack feasted on chicken salad sandwiches, corn chips, and nectarines in the peaceful solitude of Jerod's Island.

____ After a short nap the boys explored the island from end to end and had just enough time for a quick swim before paddling the canoe back to the dock on the east shore of the lake.

_1_ The three friends packed the picnic basket and looked for suntan lotion and mosquito repellent.

____ Stuffed from their lunch the boys fell asleep in the warm sand of the island's beach.

____ Then the boys carefully loaded their gear before paddling the canoe to the island in the center of the lake.

Name_____

Aunt Elsie's Chocolate Cake

Here are eight statements about *Aunt Elsie's Chocolate Cake.* The statements, however, are not listed in the proper order. By reading the statements carefully, you can determine in what sequence they should appear. Once you have decided on the correct order, number the statements to show the correct sequence.

____ When you are ready to mix the batter, you first cream together the shortening, sugar, eggs, milk, and vanilla.

____ When all the ingredients have been added and the batter is mixed, divide it into the two cake pans.

____ Set out the mixer, the recipe, and all the ingredients before you do anything else.

____ When the cake is finished baking, take it out of the oven and cool the cake at least thirty minutes before removing from pans.

____ Put the pans full of batter on the middle shelf of the oven and set the timer for 35 minutes.

____ Pre-heat the oven to 350 degrees and grease and flour two cake pans before you begin to mix the batter.

____ After 35 minutes, test the cake for doneness by inserting a toothpick in the center.

____ After creaming the first ingredients, sift together the flour, cocoa, baking powder, salt, and cream of tartar and add the dry ingredients to the batter.

Name_____

Mrs. Bluejay's Blackberry Cobbler

Here are eight statements about *Mrs. Bluejay's Blackberry Cobbler.*
However, the statements are not listed in the proper order. By
reading the statements carefully, you can determine in what
sequence they should appear. Once you have decided on the correct
order, number the statements to show the correct sequence.

____ As Clara was looking through her recipes trying to find something
special, her friend Chester Chipmunk dropped by.

____ The next morning Clara and Chester set off again with pails and
baskets to try the berry patch near Farmer Carter's pasture.
When they arrived they found Sylvester Bear and his cubs just
leaving and the briars were picked completely bare.

____ That evening, the smell of blackberry cobbler filled the forest
near Clara's oak tree, and Clara and Chester enjoyed the
delicious result of their determination and work.

____ One morning Clara Bluejay awoke with a taste for something
special. "What shall I make that's special?" she wondered aloud.

____ The third morning the determined bluejay set off again
accompanied by her neighbor the chipmunk. They found the
berry briars beside Lady's Slipper Brook bent to the ground under
the weight of ripe, juicy blackberries.

____ "Look no further," said Chester. "I know what you can make,
Clara. Susan Crow told me that the blackberries are ripe. You can
make one of your famous cobblers."

____ When they arrived at Fawn Ridge they discovered all the berries
were green—much too green for cobbler.

____ "Blackberries," cawed Clara. "We will go this very morning to
pick." So Clara and Chester set off to the berry patch atop Fawn
Ridge.

Name _____

Cornelius

Here are eleven statements about *Cornelius.* The statements, however, are not listed in the proper order. By reading the statements carefully, you can determine in what sequence they should appear. Once you have decided on the correct order, number the statements to indicate the correct sequence.

____ In three days the seed grew into a tall stalk.

____ The lady went into her garden and sang a lullaby that Mama Michi had taught her to the ear of corn atop the stalk.

____ There once was a lady who wanted a child.

____ The lady was so happy at seeing this beautiful boy no bigger than an ear of corn that tears of joy flowed down her face.

____ Suddenly, after the kiss, the husks fell open and there stood a beautiful little boy with hair as soft and pale as corn silks and with eyes as bright and blue as cornflowers.

____ The lady had her servant take her deep into the bayou country to visit an old conjurer called Mama Michi.

____ After she sang the lullaby seven times, the lady gently kissed the green ear of corn.

____ When the lady returned home after seeing Mama Michi, she planted the grain of corn in her rose garden.

____ "Don't cry, Mother," said the beautiful child. "I am your son, Cornelius."

____ Mama Michi gave the lady a magic grain of corn in exchange for three silver coins.

____ On the sixth day a large ear of corn appeared atop the stalk.

Name_____

Cheeper-Peeper

Here are twelve statements about *Cheeper-Peeper.* The statements, however, are not listed in the proper order. By reading the statements carefully, you can determine in what sequence they should appear. Once you have decided on the correct order, number the statements to show the correct order.

____ After searching and searching along the log, Peeper began to grow worried. What if Cheeper was lost or perhaps gobbled up by a hungry snake?

____ "You peep to ten," said Cheeper, as he reached the ground "and I'll go hide."

____ Peeper hopped off in the direction of his twin's voice.

____ Peeper was so worried that he sat on a velvety toadstool and began to cry. "Pee-ee-ee-eep," sobbed the tiny tree frog.

____ Once there were twin tree frogs named Peeper and Cheeper.

____ When Cheeper wasn't found under the green parasols of the mayapples, Peeper looked behind a large mushroom.

____ One bright April morning Peeper and Cheeper got tired of playing around the sassafras tree where their mother had instructed them to stay. They decided to play hide-and-seek down on the forest floor.

____ Peeper stopped crying when he heard a familiar "Cheeper-cheeper-cheeper-cheeper."

____ "Okay," agreed Peeper. "Peep-one, peep-two, peep-three..."

____ After counting to ten, Peeper first looked for Cheeper under the mayapple canopies.

____ Inside the cone of a nearby jack-in-the-pulpit sat Cheeper. The reunited little frogs began a happy chorus of, "Cheeper-peeper, cheeper-peeper, cheeper-peeper, cheeper-peeper."

____ After looking around the mushroom, Peeper checked all the small hiding places of a moss-covered hickory log.

Name _____

An **"all" statement** is a statement that is true for an entire group. If it is true for the group as a whole, it is true for all members of the group. **"All" statements** may say "all" or the all may be assumed.

Example:
   All flowers are pretty.
   A rose is a flower.
   So we know a rose is pretty.

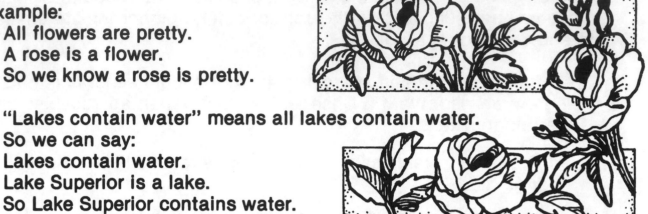

"Lakes contain water" means all lakes contain water.
So we can say:
Lakes contain water.
Lake Superior is a lake.
So Lake Superior contains water.

Read these **"all" statements** and complete the statement that follows.

1. All birds have wings.

   A sparrow is a bird.

   So a sparrow _____

2. All mammals nurse their young.

   A cow is a mammal.

   So a cow _____

3. Plants need water.

   Ivy is a plant.

   So _____

4. All plants contain chlorophyll.

   A daffodil is a plant.

   So _____

5. All dinosaurs are extinct.

   Tyrannosaurus is a dinosaur.

   So _____

6. All conifers have cones.

   A pine is a type of conifer.

   So _____

7. Fish are cold-blooded.

   Salmon are fish.

   So _____

8. All gobbles are red.

   Wurbert is a gobble.

   So _____

Name_____

You have learned that "all" statements are true for the members of a group if they are true for the group as a whole. You cannot, however, reverse "all" statements and expect them to be true. The reversals of "all" statements are not always true.

Example:
  All flowers are pretty.
  But you cannot say that all pretty things are flowers.

Read these all statements and tell whether they are true or not. Write "true" or "false" on the line following each statement.

1. **All rectangles have four sides.**

   A square is a rectangle, so a square has four sides. _____

   A rhombus has four sides, so a rhombus is a rectangle. _____

2. **All cats are mammals.**

   A horse is a mammal, so a horse is a cat. _____

   A lion is a cat, so a lion is a mammal. _____

3. **All mammals are warm-blooded.**

   A human is a mammal, so a human is warm-blooded. _____

   All warm-blooded animals are mammals. _____

4. **All dogs bark.**

   Fido is a dog, so Fido barks. _____

   All things that bark are dogs. _____

5. **All fish live in water.**

   A bass is a fish, so a bass lives in water. _____

   All things that live in water are fish. _____

33

Name_____

"No" statements are different from "all" statements in two important ways. "No" statements begin with the word "no" (or a similar word) instead of the word "all." Also "no" statements can be reversed and still be true.

Example:
   No birds are mammals.
   But we also know that no mammals are birds.

Read the following pairs of statements. Assume that the first statement is true. Decide if the second statement is true or false.

1. No mammals are cold-blooded.

   Therefore, nothing with cold blood is a mammal. _____

2. No people are fish.

   So no fish are people. _____

3. No fourth-graders are absent.

   Therefore, none of the people who are absent are in fourth grade. _____

   Here are some "no" statements. Write the reversal of each one.

4. Cars cannot fly.

   _____

5. No hippopotamuses can sing.

   _____

6. No grass is purple.

   _____

Name_____

One of the oldest of all logic problems, the **syllogism**, has three parts. The first two statements are called **premises.** The last statement is called the **conclusion.** A syllogism can be either valid (true) or invalid (not true) depending on whether the conclusion is supported by the premises.

By carefully studying the first two parts of a syllogism you should be able to determine if the third part is valid.

All cats have fur.   **premise 1**
Tigers are cats.   **premise 2**
Therefore, all tigers have fur.   **conclusion**

In this syllogism, the first two premises support the conclusion so the syllogism is said to be **valid.**

All tigers have stripes.   **premise 1**
All tigers are cats.   **premise 2**
So, all cats have stripes.   **conclusion**

In this syllogism, the first two premises do not support the conclusion so the syllogism is said to be **invalid.**

Remember that premises may be true and the conclusion still be invalid. It simply means that the information given in the premises does not support that conclusion.

Decide whether the following statements are premises or conclusions. Circle the correct label for each statement.

1. All flowers are pretty.   premise   conclusion
   Therefore, a rose is pretty.   premise   conclusion
   A rose is a flower.   premise   conclusion

2. Therefore, corn is good for you.   premise   conclusion
   All vegetables are good for you.   premise   conclusion
   Corn is a vegetable.   premise   conclusion

3. All my students are hard workers.   premise   conclusion
   Gina is one of my students.   premise   conclusion
   Therefore, Gina is a hard worker.   premise   conclusion

Name_____

For these exercises, you will be given two premises. You may assume
that all the premises are true. Try to decide if the conclusions given
are valid or invalid. After you decide whether the conclusions can be
supported by the premises, circle the correct answer.

Example: All galaxies contain stars.
 The Milky Way is a galaxy.
 Therefore, The Milky Way contains stars.   (Valid) Invalid

 All galaxies contain stars.
 Galaxies are big.
 Therefore, stars are big.   Valid (Invalid)

Penguins are birds.
All birds have feathers.
 1. Therefore, all birds are penguins.   valid   invalid
 2. Therefore, penguins have feathers.   valid   invalid
 3. Therefore, all birds fly.   valid   invalid

All elephants are big.
All big animals eat a lot of food.
 4. Therefore, all animals that eat a lot of food are elephants.   valid   invalid
 5. Therefore, all elephants eat a lot of food.   valid   invalid
 6. All elephants eat more than whales   valid   invalid

All birds have feathers.
All robins are birds.
 7. Therefore, all robins have feathers.   valid   invalid
 8. Therefore, no robins have feathers.   valid   invalid
 9. Therefore, all robins eat worms.   valid   invalid

All trees have bark.
An oak is a tree.
10. Therefore, an oak has bark.   valid   invalid
11. Therefore, everything with bark is a tree.   valid   invalid
12. Therefore, all trees are oaks.   valid   invalid

Name_____

In this exercise, you will be given two premises. Read each one carefully and then decide whether the conclusions are valid or invalid. After you decide whether the conclusions can be supported by the premises, circle the correct answer.

All pickles are green.
No carrots are green.
1. Therefore, no carrots are pickles.　　　valid　　invalid
2. Therefore, no pickles are carrots.　　　valid　　invalid
3. Therefore, some pickles are sour.　　　valid　　invalid

All glass is transparent.
All transparent things are fragile.
4. Therefore, all fragile things are glass.　　　valid　　invalid
5. Therefore, all glass is fragile.　　　valid　　invalid
6. Therefore, some glass is not fragile.　　　valid　　invalid
7. Therefore, all fragile things are transparent.　　　valid　　invalid

All gold is valuable.
Nothing valuable is cheap.
8. Therefore, no gold is cheap.　　　valid　　invalid
9. Therefore, nothing cheap is gold.　　　valid　　invalid
10. Therefore, some gold is mined.　　　valid　　invalid

All flowers are pretty.
Violets are flowers
11. Therefore, violets are pretty.　　　valid　　invalid
12. Therefore, all pretty things are flowers.　　　valid　　invalid
13. Therefore, violets have petals.　　　valid　　invalid

Name _____

In this exercise, you will be given two premises. Read each one carefully and then decide whether the conclusions are valid or invalid. After you decide whether the conclusions can be supported by the premises, circle the correct answer.

All frogs are amphibians
All amphibians swim.
1. Therefore, some frogs hop.   valid   invalid
2. Therefore, all frogs swim.   valid   invalid
3. Therefore, all amphibians are frogs.   valid   invalid
4. Therefore, no frogs can swim.   valid   invalid

All flowers are fragrant.
All fragrant things attract bees.
5. Therefore, all flowers attract bees.   valid   invalid
6. Therefore, no bees are attracted to flowers.   valid   invalid
7. Therefore, some flowers are pink.   valid   invalid

All teachers are intelligent.
All writers are intelligent.
8. Therefore, all writers are teachers.   valid   invalid
9. Therefore, all teachers are writers.   valid   invalid
10. Therefore, some teachers are writers.   valid   invalid

We go to school each weekday.
Wednesday is a weekday.
11. Therefore, every weekday is Wednesday.   valid   invalid
12. Therefore, we go to school on Wednesday.   valid   invalid
13. Therefore, Wednesday is the best day of the week. valid   invalid

Name_____

In this exercise, you will be given two premises. Read each one carefully and then decide on a conclusion that would be valid, that is, a conclusion that would be supported by the two premises.

1. All sheep eat grass.
   All grasses are plants.
   Therefore, _____

2. All horses are animals.
   No animals are vegetables.
   Therefore, _____

3. Mrs. Smith does not like cats.
   Mischief is a cat.
   Therefore, _____

4. My dad's old car is a wreck.
   All wrecks should be sent to the dump.
   Therefore, _____

5. I like anything that is chocolate.
   Fudge is chocolate.
   Therefore, _____

6. All teachers like children.
   Mr. Muffet teaches 4th grade.
   Therefore, _____

7. No ducks are purple.
   Daffy is a duck.
   Therefore, _____

8. All plants have roots.
   No things with roots can walk.
   Therefore, _____

Name _____

In this exercise, you will be given two premises. Read each one and then write one valid conclusion for the premises.

1. Some children are blond.
   All blonds are pretty.
   Therefore, _____

2. All candy is sweet.
   All sweet things taste good.
   Therefore, _____

3. No dogs are purple.
   All prickly things are purple.
   Therefore, _____

4. All baseball players can throw a ball.
   Julie plays second base on our team.
   Therefore, _____

5. All rich people have a lot of money.
   My uncle is rich.
   Therefore, _____

Write two syllogisms of your own. For each one, write two premises and a conclusion that is supported by the two premises.

6. premise 1 _____
   premise 2 _____
   conclusion _____

7. premise 1 _____
   premise 2 _____
   conclusion _____

Name_____

An **"if-then" statement** has two parts: a **condition** and a **result**. They are related in such a way that if the one thing happens, then the other event will also happen. The word "if" (or some similar word) must appear in the sentence. The word "then" may appear or may be left out and just be taken for granted.

Example:
    If it rains, then I will get wet.
    If I wear my good shoes, mother will get mad.

The following examples are missing either the "if" part or the "then" part of the statements. Fill in the blanks to make complete "if-then" statements.

1. If _____ , then we will win the game.

2. If _____ , then I will have to go to the store.

3. If today is Wednesday, then _____.

4. If you miss ten on your spelling test, _____.

5. If _____ , then you are in 4th grade.

6. If you like dogs, then _____.

Name_____

You have learned that an "if-then" statement has two parts. The condition is stated in the "If" part of the statement, and the result contains the word "then." If the condition part of the statement is met, you can conclude the result will happen.
Example:
    If it rains, then we must have clouds.
    It is raining.
    Therefore, we can conclude that we have clouds.

You cannot, however, reverse an "if-then" statement and assume it is true. If the result takes place, it does not mean that the conditions have been met.

Example:
    If it rains, I will bring by umbrella.
    I brought my umbrella.
    But you **cannot** conclude from this that it is raining.

Complete these "if-then" statements so they are true.

1. If it is hot, then Carla will go to the pool.

   It is hot, so _____

2. If it snows, we will not have to go to school.

   It is snowing, so _____

3. If the tree is at least 10 feet tall, then we will cut it down.

   The tree is 12 feet tall, so _____

4. If you get all the answers right, you will get an A on the test.

   You got 100 % correct, so _____

5. If Carmen goes, then Josh will go too.

   Carmen is going, so _____

6. If this is a triangle, then it has three sides.

   This is a triangle, so _____

Name_____

Read these "if-then" statements carefully. Then decide if the
conclusion is correct. If it is, write "yes." If it is not, write "no."

1. If Joy reads at least 15 books, she will get an award.
   Joy reads 16 books.
   Can you conclude Joy will get an award? _____

2. If we go on vacation, we will put the dog in the kennel.
   The dog is in the kennel.
   Can you conclude we are on vacation? _____

3. If it rains, the ball game will be cancelled.
   It is raining.
   Can you conclude the ball game will be cancelled? _____

4. If Mark rides the bus, then he will get home by 4 o'clock.
   Mark rides the bus.
   Can you conclude he will get home by 4 o'clock? _____

5. If you inhale pepper, then you will sneeze.
   You are sneezing.
   Can you conclude you inhaled pepper? _____

6. If someone rings the door bell, then Scuffy will bark.
   Scuffy is barking.
   Can you conclude that someone rang the door bell? _____

7. If we win the game, then the coach will buy us pizza.
   We won the game.
   Can you conclude that the coach will buy us pizza? _____

8. If John sits on the balloon, then it will pop.
   The balloon pops.
   Can you you conclude that John sat on the balloon? _____

9. If this is the first day in October, then it is my birthday.
   Today is October 1.
   Can you conclude that it is my birthday? _____

Name_____

The Pyramid

Connie, Virginia, Steve, Randy, Valery, and Karen are cheerleaders at Southside Junior High. One of their routines calls for them to form a pyramid with three people on the bottom, two people in the middle tier, and one person on top.

Read the clues and then put everyone in their proper position. Label each circle with one cheerleader's name.

Clues:
1. Connie is between Steve and Randy.

2. Virginia is on top of Connie and Steve but helping to support Valery.

3. Karen is on the right side of the pyramid.

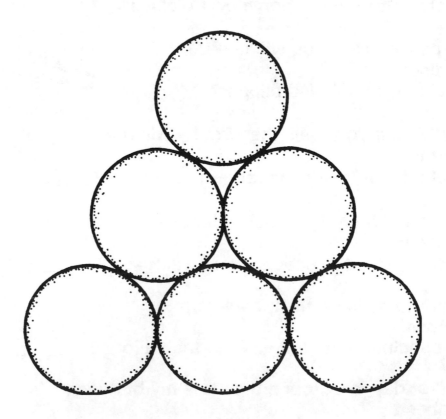

Name_____

The Train

Keith is a radio dispatcher for KRGRR. He is expecting an eastbound freight train made up of twelve cars. Uncouple the clues and decide what order the cars are in. To help you the train is divided into three parts.

1. The locomotive is pulling the whole train. The boxcar of wheat is between the cattle car and the refrigerated car of potatoes. The refrigerated car is not coupled to the locomotive.

2. The flatcar loaded with generators is between the gondola car of logs and hopper car of coal. The coal hopper car is between the tanker car of corn syrup and flatcar with generators. The gondola car with logs and the flatcar with generators are both ahead of the hopper car with coal and the tanker of syrup.

3. The caboose is the last car on the train. The piggyback loaded with new cars and the boxcar loaded with appliances are not next to the caboose. The piggyback of new cars is between the soybeans and appliances.

1. _____   9. _____

2. _____   10. _____

3. _____   11. _____

4. _____   12. _____

5. _____

6. _____

7. _____

8. _____

Name_____

The Darkroom

Madge found a strip of six 35mm negatives that had been lost. She knew they were snapshots of her vacation trip. Develop the clues so you can tell which picture is which.

Clues

1. Grandpa Frank's picture is between the picture of Uncle Jesse and Aunt Betty and the one of Pike's Peak.

2. The picture of Uncle Wendell's family is between the snapshot of Pike's Peak and the picture of the Colorado River.

3. The picture of the Pacific Ocean is on one end of the strip and is next to the picture of the Colorado River.

4. The first snapshot is of people rather than scenery.

1._____

2._____

3._____

4._____

5._____

6._____

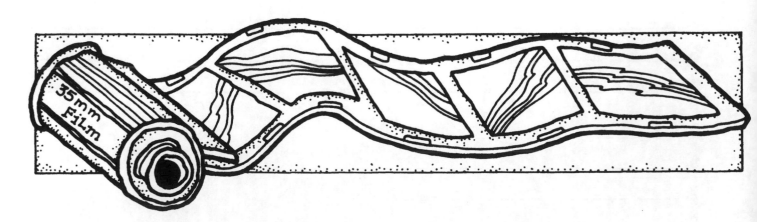

Name _____

Pizza Party

Heidi, John, Susan, and Dianne decided to celebrate by ordering a pizza at their favorite pizzeria. In addition to the regular toppings, each friend ordered something special on their quarter of the pizza. Give the clues a toss and see if you can figure out who ordered pepperoni, black olives, mushrooms, and anchovies.

Clues

1. Heidi, and the girl ordering pepperoni, and the boy ordering anchovies all played video games while they waited for their pizza to bake.

2. Dianne hates pepperoni and Heidi hates mushrooms.

	pepperoni	black olives	mushrooms	anchovies
Heidi				
John				
Susan				
Dianne				

Name_____

The Frog Jumping Contest

Four friends, Lauren, Matthew, Robby, and Juan, entered their pet
frogs in the annual Frog Jumping Contest. The four frogs' final
distances were two feet, three feet, four feet, and six feet. Hop to it
and use the clues below and see if you can figure out how far each
person's frog jumped.

Clues

1. Matthew's frog jumped further that Juan's and Lauren's but not as
   far as Robby's.

2. Matthew's frog jumped twice as far as Juan's.

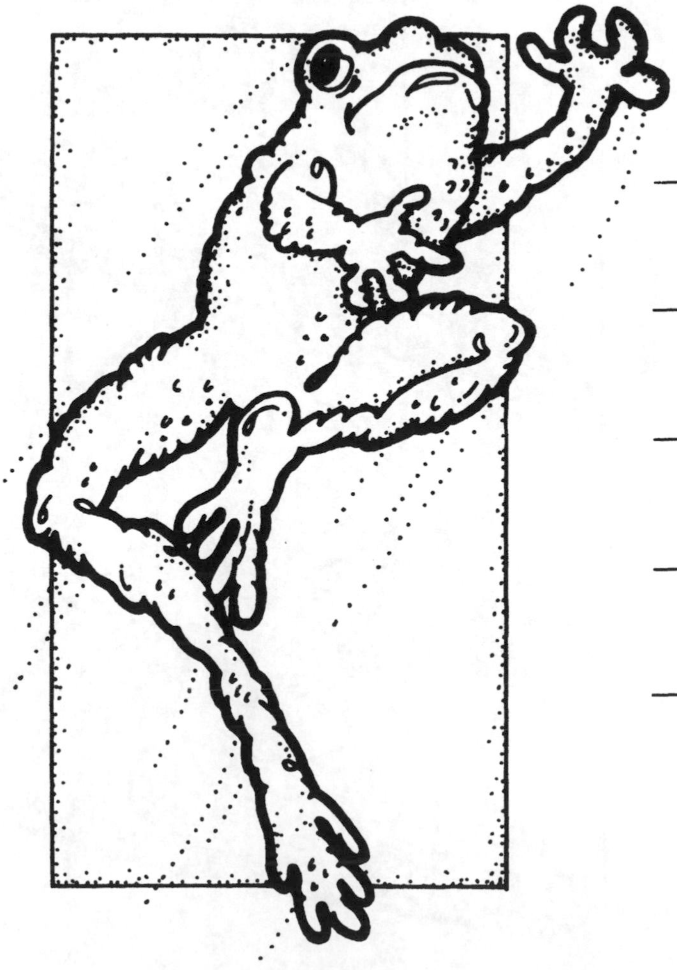

	Lauren	Matthew	Robby	Juan
2 feet				
3 feet				
4 feet				
6 feet				

Name_____

Taking Turns at the Post Office

Mr. McGuire, Mrs. Jesson, and Mrs. Gibson arrived at the post office within minutes of each other. Each took a number (137, 138, 139) to be waited on. Each person had one errand to do at the post office. One person needed to buy stamps, one came to mail a parcel, and one needed to pick up a letter. Sort through the clues and stamp out the solution to who did what and in what order.

Clues

1. The man buying stamps was waited on before the lady mailing a parcel but after Mrs. Jesson.

2. One person waited 2 minutes to be waited on, one waited 4 minutes, and one waited 5 minutes.

	buy stamps	mail parcel	pick up letter	137	138	139
Mr. McGuire						
Mrs. Jesson						
Mrs. Gibson						
137						
138						
139						

Name_____

Wishing for Rides

Chad, Bob, Susan, and Jack wished for rides on a motor boat, a hot-air balloon, a helicopter, and a fire engine. Read the clues to see if you can determine who wanted to ride on what.

Clues

1. Chad, the girl who wants to ride in a hot-air balloon, and the boy who wants to ride on a fire engine all want to leave early Saturday morning.

2. Chad and Jack get seasick on boats.

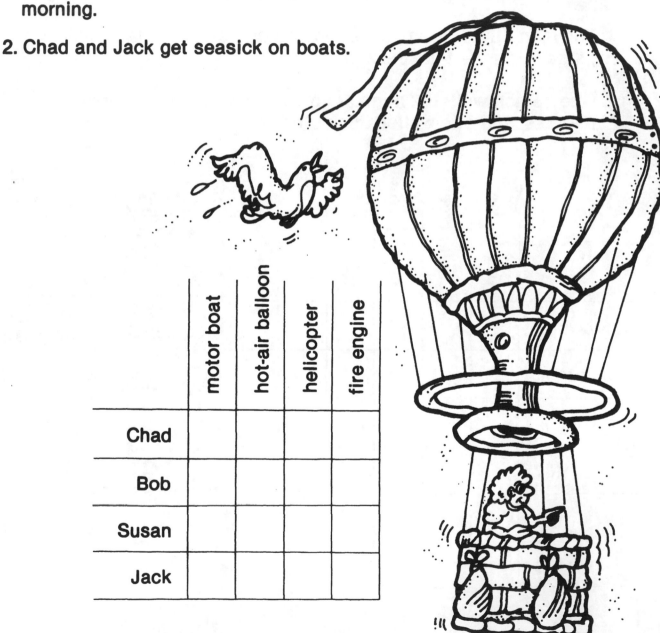

	motor boat	hot-air balloon	helicopter	fire engine
Chad				
Bob				
Susan				
Jack				

Name_____

Spring Bulbs

Thelma, Jim, Mary, and Randy volunteered to plant spring-blooming bulbs around the gazebo of their neighbor's yard. Jonquils, hyacinths, tulips, and crocuses were planted. Seventy-five, eighty-one, eighty-six, and ninety bulbs were planted of the different species. Dig through the clues and see if you can unearth who planted what and how many bulbs each person planted.

Clues

1. Thelma, the boy planting jonquils, and the girl who plants 86 bulbs all took turns with the wheelbarrow and mulch.

2. Jim planted more bulbs than the girl planting hyacinths but fewer than the girl planting tulips and the boy planting crocus bulbs.

	jonquils	hyacinths	tulips	crocuses	75	81	86	90
Thelma								
Jim								
Mary								
Randy								
75								
81								
86								
90								

Name_____

Aunt Sophie's Fruit Salad

At a recent family get-together, Patricia, Ronald, Tonia, and William were all in the kitchen helping Aunt Sophie prepare her famous fruit salad. The four cousins helped slice bananas, dice apples, pit cherries, and halve strawberries. The recipe called for 1½ cups, 2 cups, 2½ cups, and 3 cups of these fruits. Now pare away at the clues and see who prepared each fruit and how much fruit each person made for the salad.

Clues

1. Patricia prepared more than the boy pitting cherries and the girl slicing bananas, but less than Ronald.

2. The recipe called for ½ cup more strawberries than cherries.

3. Ronald did not halve strawberries.

	bananas	apples	cherries	strawberries	1½ cups	2 cups	2½ cups	3 cups
Patricia								
Ronald								
Tonia								
William								
1½ cups								
2 cups								
2½ cups								
3 cups								

Name_____

In each set of words the same letter has been replaced by a □ to form a stairway. On the line following each set write what the □ stands for. Remember the letter you pick to replace the □ must form a real word with each member of the set.

Example:
□cho
s□at
fe□t
hav□
□ stands for **e.**

1. □ood
   e□es
   fa□n
   cro□
   □ stands for ____

2. □ond
   s□ell
   wi□e
   lea□
   □ stands for ____

3. lav□
   to□d
   f□de
   □ces
   □ stands for ____

4. bus□
   cr□
   r□e
   □elp
   □ stands for ____

5. □ews
   k□ee
   lo□g
   fer□
   □ stands for ____

6. □aid
   e□pire
   bu□p
   loo□
   □ stands for ____

7. □oor
   e□dy
   ri□e
   len□
   □ stands for ____

8. □eaf
   i□ea
   ru□e
   woo□
   □ stands for ____

9. ecr□
   ch□rn
   s□re
   □pset
   □ stands for ____

10. pea□h
    de□k
    e□ho
    □ool
    □ stands for ____

11. □eed
    k□ow
    wi□d
    soo□
    □ stands for ____

12. □air
    a□ar
    sa□e
    cuf□
    □ stands for ____

Name _____

In each set of words the same letter has been replaced by a □ to form a stairway. On the line following each set write what the □ stands for. Remember the letter you pick to replace the □ must form a real word with each member of the set.

Example: □ail
         f□ay
         to□n
         pur□
         □ stands for **r**

1. □umb
   i□le
   ki□s
   sle□
   □ stands for ____

2. □ope
   f□ee
   cu□e
   hai□
   □ stands for ____

3. lim□
   tu□s
   o□ey
   □oil
   □ stands for ____

4. roa□
   ti□y
   a□opt
   □ate
   □ stands for ____

5. □ulp
   s□an
   lo□e
   rea□
   □ stands for ____

6. □uck
   a□pen
   di□h
   mos□
   □ stands for ____

7. □and
   lo□t
   wi□h
   bas□
   □ stands for ____

8. □ole
   s□ip
   be□ave
   das□
   □ stands for ____

9. dee□
   ca□e
   s□are
   □eak
   □ stands for ____

10. den□
    fl□
    m□th
    □ule
    □ stands for ____

11. □ear
    a□vise
    ro□e
    fle□
    □ stands for ____

12. □ond
    s□y
    ma□s
    lum□
    □ stands for ____

Name_____

In each set of words the same letter has been replaced by a □ to form a stairway. On the line following each set write what the stands for. Remember the letter you pick to replace the □ must form a real word with each member of the set.

Example: □oap
         u□er
         no□e
         bas□
         □ stands for **s**

1. □hat
   a□ry
   do□n
   gro□
   □ stands for ___

2. □hen
   s□un
   da□e
   gis□
   □ stands for ___

3. hid□
   sh□d
   f□ed
   □ggs
   □ stands for ___

4. eas□
   pr□
   t□pe
   □oke
   □ stands for ___

5. □uma
   s□eak
   ty□e
   kee□
   □ stands for ___

6. □oll
   t□ee
   ba□k
   poo□
   □ stands for ___

7. □rag
   a□ds
   ro□e
   len□
   □ stands for ___

8. □ala
   a□ate
   pa□e
   ban□
   □ stands for ___

9. clu□
   tu□e
   o□ey
   □all
   □ stands for ___

10. twi□e
    fa□e
    a□es
    □ame
    □ stands for ___

11. □act
    o□fer
    li□e
    dea□
    □ stands for ___

12. □iss
    s□id
    ta□e
    boo□
    □ stands for ___

Name_____

In each set of words the same letter has been replaced by a □ to form a stairway. On the line following each set write what the □ stands for. Remember the letter you pick to replace the □ must form a real word with each member of the set.

Example: dar□
          de□t
          o□ce
          □ail
          □ stands for **n**

1. □not
  s□im
  la□e
  lic□
  □ stands for ___

2. □ime
  e□ch
  ki□e
  tes□
  □ stands for ___

3. dea□
  se□f
  b□ew
  □amb
  □ stands for ___

4. oli□e
  li□e
  o□er
  □isa
  □ stands for ___

5. □oon
  k□ife
  we□t
  wor□
  □ stands for ___

6. □ore
  i□port
  co□b
  cal□
  □ stands for ___

7. □are
  a□end
  ar□y
  ste□
  □ stands for ___

8. □ind
  a□ford
  so□t
  cal□
  □ stands for ___

9. boi□
  ti□t
  c□ad
  □ook
  □ stands for ___

10. bea□
  li□e
  a□ong
  □ist
  □ stands for ___

11. □eaf
  c□ad
  be□l
  dia□
  □ stands for ___

12. □ast
  a□bush
  ca□e
  ato□
  □ stands for ___

Name_____

The object of these puzzles is to transform the word on the top line into the word on the bottom line by changing only one letter at a time. To solve the puzzles you must follow these rules:

1. Change only one of the letters in each move.
2. Each new transformation must be a real word.
3. Change each letter only once.
4. Use only three turns to reach the word at the bottom.

Example: clip
slip
ship
shop

Since these puzzles are much more difficult than they appear, working them on scrap paper first is recommended.

1. fade	2. band	3. feed	4. stop	5. sick
_____	_____	_____	_____	_____
_____	_____	_____	_____	_____
mole	seed	step	chip	tact

6. year	7. yard	8. dock	9. curb	10. fact
_____	_____	_____	_____	_____
_____	_____	_____	_____	_____
deed	born	core	lard	case

Name_____

Many times a missing word can be filled in by using the clues from the context of the sentence. The same word is missing in all four sentences. Read each sentence carefully to discover the missing word. Remember the missing word must fit into each sentence in the set and the sentences must make sense.

Set 1

Sarah has dealt me five cards of the same _____.

The cleaner delivered my blue _____ on Tuesday.

If my plans _____ you, we can catch a plane tonight.

Our _____ will be heard by the judge on the nineteenth.

Set 2

The forest _____ has been caused by a careless camper.

They were counting down to _____ the rocket.

The foreman was forced to _____ the woman because of repeated tardiness.

The _____ engine raced down the street.

Set 3

Do we have a _____ to take the river cruise?

Grandma always makes _____ bread for the holidays.

Today's _____ is Tuesday January 22.

Bob gave his _____ a gardenia corsage before the dance.

Set 4

The campers watched the _____ of dawn on a cliff overlooking Current River.

Would you like me to _____ the fireplace fire?

This morning I feel as _____ as a feather.

The princess wore a _____ blue suit to the ceremony.

Name_____

Guess-a-Word

For each of the problems in this activity you must use the clues for four smaller words to help you discover the main word that is made of the letters in each of the smaller words. The clues for the smaller words are given in terms of the letters and their positions in the main word.

1. A nine-letter word that is a holiday

$\underline{}_1 \underline{}_2 \underline{}_3 \underline{}_4 \underline{}_5 \underline{}_6 \underline{}_7 \underline{}_8 \underline{}_9$

$\underline{}_3 \underline{a}_2 \underline{}_6 \underline{}_9$ grass

$\underline{w}_6 \underline{}_1 \underline{}_7 \underline{}_8 \underline{}_4$ part of a car

$\underline{}_4 \underline{}_5 \underline{}_6$ not high

$\underline{}_3 \underline{}_7 \underline{}_2 \underline{}_9$ not fat

2. A ten-letter word that is a sport

$\underline{}_1 \underline{}_2 \underline{}_3 \underline{}_4 \underline{}_5 \underline{}_6 \underline{}_7 \underline{}_8 \underline{}_9 \underline{}_{10}$

$\underline{b}_1 \underline{}_5 \underline{}_2 \underline{}_6$ to strike

$\underline{}_7 \underline{}_2 \underline{}_3 \underline{}_5$ lowest part

$\underline{}_6 \underline{}_2 \underline{}_9 \underline{}_{10}$ not short

$\underline{s}_3 \underline{}_4 \underline{}_2 \underline{}_6 \underline{}_5$ shoe with rollers

3. An eight-letter word that is a flower

$\underline{}_1 \underline{}_2 \underline{}_3 \underline{}_4 \underline{}_5 \underline{}_6 \underline{}_7 \underline{}_8$

$\underline{n}_6 \underline{}_8 \underline{}_1$ scold or complain

$\underline{}_4 \underline{}_5 \underline{}_6$ a small room

$\underline{}_3 \underline{}_5 \underline{}_2 \underline{}_4$ decipher written words

$\underline{}_4 \underline{}_7 \underline{}_1$ excavate

4. A eleven-letter word that is a festivity

$\underline{}_1 \underline{}_2 \underline{}_3 \underline{}_4 \underline{}_5 \underline{}_6 \underline{}_7 \underline{}_8 \underline{}_9 \underline{}_{10} \underline{}_{11}$

$\underline{b}_5 \underline{}_6 \underline{}_7 \underline{}_{11}$ outer husk of cereal

$\underline{}_5 \underline{}_2 \underline{}_7 \underline{}_8$ mix rapidly

$\underline{c}_1 \underline{}_4 \underline{}_6 \underline{}_2 \underline{}_7 \underline{}_3$ breakfast food

$\underline{}_5 \underline{}_{10} \underline{}_9 \underline{}_3$ cook by high temperature

Answers

Lesson 1
1. all are colors
2. all are shapes or all are polygons
3. all are units of measure
4. all are countries in Europe
5. all are made of paper and used for writing
6. all are used for cutting
7. all are white and used for cooking
8. all are flavors
9. all are types of trees
10. all are cities in the United States
11. all are containers
12. all are sweet things to eat

Lesson 2
1. any type of grain
2. any piece of clothing
3. liquid to drink, beverages
4. days of the week
5. birds
6. modes of transportation
7. things used in a classroom
8. things that are green
9. fruits, things with seeds
10. holidays
11. girls' names

Lesson 3
1. things with pits
2. fruits, things with seeds
3. sports played with balls
4. green things
5. things that are spheres
6. sweet things
7. things with four wheels
8. weather conditions
9. yellow things
10. things that grow underground
11. insects
12. things that are brown

Lesson 4
answers will vary

Lesson 5
1. things that are brown
2. things that are round
3. things that are yellow
4. things that can fly
5. inside things

Lesson 6
1. N, vowels
2. robin, mammals
3. Ted, girls' names
4. 7, even numbers
5. milk, things found in a desk
6. potato, fruits
7. banana, things that are red or round
8. O, letters made with straight lines

Lesson 7
1. one dot, even
2. ⊢ , y-shaped
3. six-dot shape, made of 3 parts
4. circle, made of straight lines
5. tired, senses
6. moon, planets
7. pizza, sweet things
8. pepper, white things
9. 15 cents, single coins

Lesson 8
1. c
2. b
3. a
4. a
5. b
6. c

Lesson 9
1. a
2. c
3. a
4. c
5. b
6. b

Lesson 10
1. d	6. d
2. c	7. a
3. d	8. b
4. b	9. a
5. b	10. c

Lesson 11
1. b	6. c
2. d	7. c
3. c	8. b
4. d	9. d
5. a	10. b

Lesson 12
1. d	6. a
2. c	7. c
3. d	8. a
4. b	9. c
5. d	10. d

Lesson 13
1. c	6. c
2. a	7. c
3. b	8. d
4. c	9. b
5. a	10. c

Lesson 14

1. c	6. d
2. a	7. b
3. c	8. b
4. a	9. c
5. c	10. b

Lesson 15

1. c	6. b
2. c	7. c
3. d	8. a
4. c	9. b
5. b	10. c

Lesson 16

1. c	6. b
2. a	7. c
3. d	8. d
4. a	9. c
5. c	10. a

Lesson 17

1. c	6. b
2. d	7. a
3. c	8. c
4. c	9. d
5. d	10. a

Lesson 18

1. any reasonable answer

Lesson 19

1. b	9. a
2. d	10. c
3. c	11. d
4. b	12. a
5. b	13. c
6. c	14. b
7. a	
8. b	

Lesson 20

1. c	7. c
2. b	8. b
3. b	9. a
4. a	10. a
5. c	11. c
6. c	12. d

Lesson 21

3, 5, 1, 4, 2

Lesson 22

3, 5, 1, 8, 6, 2, 7, 4

Lesson 23

2, 6, 8, 1, 7, 3, 5, 4

Lesson 24

5, 7, 1, 10, 9, 2, 8, 4, 11, 3, 6

Lesson 25

8, 3, 11, 9, 1, 6, 2, 10, 4, 5, 12, 7

Lesson 26

1. has wings
2. nurses its young
3. ivy needs water
4. a daffodil contains chlorophyll
5. tyrannosaurus is extinct
6. a pine has cones
7. salmon are cold-blooded
8. Wurbert is red

Lesson 27

1. true, false
2. false, true
3. true, false
4. true, false
5. true, false

Lesson 28

1. true
2. true
3. true
4. No flying things are cars.
5. No singers are hippotamuses.
6. No purple things are grass.

Lesson 29

1. premise
   conclusion
   premise
2. conclusion
   premise
   premise
3. premise
   premise
   conclusion

Lesson 30

1. Invalid	9. Invalid
2. Valid	10. Valid
3. Invalid	11. Invalid
4. Invalid	12. Invalid
5. Valid	
6. Invalid	
7. Valid	
8. Invalid	

Lesson 31
1. Valid	7. Invalid
2. Valid	8. Valid
3. Invalid	9. Valid
4. Invalid	10. Invalid
5. Valid	11. Valid
6. Invalid	12. Invalid
	13. Invalid

Lesson 32
1. Invalid	7. Invalid
2. Valid	8. Invalid
3. Invalid	9. Invalid
4. Invalid	10. Invalid
5. Valid	11. Invalid
6. Invalid	12. Valid
	13. Invalid

Lesson 33
1. Sheep eat plants.
2. A horse is not a vegetable.
3. Mrs. Smith does not like Mischief.
4. My dad's car should be sent to the dump.
5. I like fudge.
6. Mr. Muffet likes children.
7. Daffy is not purple.
8. Plants cannot walk.

Lesson 34
Answers will vary but some possible valid answers are:
1. Some children are pretty.
2. All candy tastes good.
3. No dogs are prickly.
4. Julie can throw a ball.
5. My uncle has a lot of money.
6. answers will vary
7. answers will vary

Lesson 35
Answers will vary

Lesson 36
1. Carla will go to the pool.
2. we will not have to go to school.
3. we will cut down the tree.
4. you will get an A on the test.
5. Josh is going also.
6. It has three sides.

Lesson 37
1. yes	6. no
2. no	7. yes
3. yes	8. no
4. yes	9. yes
5. no	

Lesson 38
Valery

Virginia   Karen

Steve   Connie   Randy

Lesson 39
1. locomotive
2. cattle car
3. boxcar (wheat)
4. refrigerator (potatoes)

5. gondola car (logs)
6. flatcar (generators)
7. hopper car (coal)
8. tanker car (corn syrup)

9. box car (appliances)
10. piggyback (new cars)
11. soybeans
12. caboose

Lesson 40
1. Uncle Jesse and Aunt Betty
2. Grandpa Frank
3. Pike's Peak
4. Uncle Wendell's family
5. Colorado River
6. Pacific Ocean

Lesson 41
Heidi - black olives
John - anchovies
Susan - pepperoni
Dianne - mushrooms

Lesson 42
Lauren - 3 feet
Matthew - 4 feet
Robby - 6 feet
Juan - 2 feet

Lesson 43
Mr. McGuire - stamps, 138
Mrs. Jesson - letter, 137
Mrs. Gibson - parcel, 139

Lesson 44
Chad - helicopter
Bob - motor boat
Susan - hot air balloon
Jack - fire engine

Lesson 45
Thelma - hyacinths, 75
Jim - jonquils, 81
Mary - tulips, 86
Randy - crocuses, 90

Lesson 46
Patricia - strawberries, 2½ cups
Ronald - apples, 3 cups
Tonia - bananas, 1½ cups
William - cherries, 2 cups

Lesson 47
1. w   7. d
2. p   8. d
3. a   9. u
4. y   10. c
5. n   11. n
6. m   12. f

Lesson 48
1. d   7. s
2. r   8. h
3. b   9. p
4. d   10. y
5. p   11. d
6. s   12. p

Lesson 49
1. w   7. d
2. t   8. g
3. e   9. b
4. y   10. c
5. p   11. f
6. r   12. k

Lesson 50
1. k   7. m
2. t   8. f
3. l   9. l
4. v   10. m
5. n   11. l
6. m   12. m

Lesson 51
fade	band	feed	stop	sick	year	yard	dock	curb	fact
made	sand	seed	shop	sack	dear	yarn	cock	curd	fast
mode	send	seep	ship	tack	deer	barn	cork	card	cast
mole	seed	step	chip	tact	deed	born	core	lard	case

Lesson 52
1. suit   2. fire
3. date   4. light

Lesson 53
1. halloween   3. gardenia
   lawn   nag
   wheel   den
   low   read
   lean   dig

2. basketball   4. celebration
   beat   bran
   base   beat
   tall   cereal
   skate   boil

Lesson 54
1. elephant   3. astronomy
   leap   atom
   tape   moon
   heel   story
   then   moan

2. valentine   4. democracy
   tale   roam
   van   cream
   nine   race
   vent   yard

Printed in the United States
by Baker & Taylor Publisher Services